THE *S.H.E.* GUIDE

(See Her Evolve)

SEASON OF INTENTION

THE *S.H.E.* GUIDE

(See Her Evolve)

A transformative seasonal journal for women of color to create a meaningful & thriving lifestyle.

KENYA MCGUIRE JOHNSON

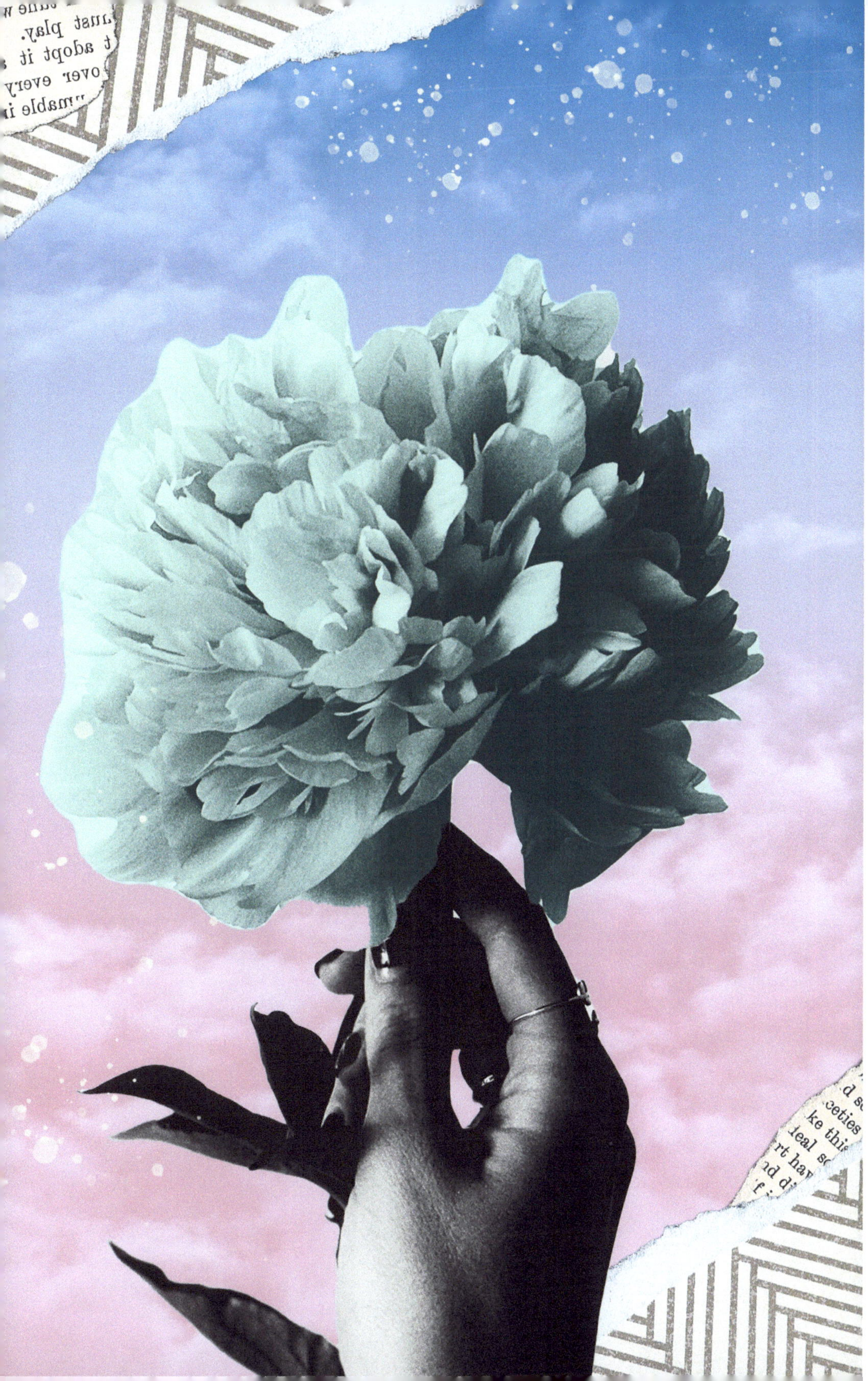

INTRODUCTION:
PURPOSE & HOW TO USE THE
S.H.E. GUIDE TO THRIVE

Congratulations! If you are reading this, you have decided to choose you! Despite the many roles, responsibilities and obligations you are tethered to, you have a personal awareness of your needs. You recognize that, in spite of the many activities you do for others, you are the center of your own life. The thought of focusing on yourself is now being understood personally as a courageous act of love. It feels more urgent and you're beginning to shed feelings of guilt for wanting to focus on your mental & emotional health. In addition, you are learning that choosing yourself first is not selfish; in fact, you are realizing that if you don't choose yourself first, who will?

Depending on your current stage of life, you are having more "a-ha" moments about your personal lifestyle. You value your inner voice and it's telling you that it's time to make changes so that you choose yourself in a healthy, helpful and consistent manner. As a result, you are likely to be experiencing at least one or more of the following scenarios:

Scenario 1: *You are arriving at a place in life where you want to feel empowered, aligned and in flow with your dreams and desires. You no longer want to equate your worth to what you have or don't have. You no longer have the energy to waste on worrying about what others think about you nor do you care about what others say about you behind your back. You can no longer push the "pause" button on your personal growth and satisfaction to keep others comfortable. Your "people-pleasing" energy is slowly dissolving and you want to replace it with "self-pleasing" because you deserve just as much joy as you work hard to provide for others.*

Scenario 2: *You want more for your life. Despite your many successes, emptiness or stagnation is still there. You have an overall feeling of gratitude and have a sense of pride about what you have accomplished, but you don't consistently celebrate your wins. In fact, you move so quickly to take care of work responsibilities, children, spouses, partners, significant others, siblings, friends, aging parents, co-workers, employees, employers, household chores, finances and a myriad of other things that you simply push through in order to conquer the next task. Birthdays and some holidays give you a slight reprieve, but even then you find yourself planning and executing so many actions that you barely remember what you did last Christmas or your previous birthday.*

Scenario 3: *You have worked hard to establish your career in a way that provides stability, yet emerging challenges, especially those that manifested during the pandemic, make you realize that your career may not be the best fit for this stage of life. What worked previously no longer feels like an appropriate match. In fact, you've out-grown many of the skills you worked hard for others to recognize. You want something different, but fear of the unknown is paralyzing at best. Your financial stability is mandatory and trying something new could potentially jeopardize many things you value. Still … your current work-life simply isn't feeding your soul the way it did in the past.*

Scenario 4: *You recently experienced a loss, and that has left you feeling anxious, depressed, lonely and/or lifeless. You appreciate that eventually you will feel better, but the loss is outweighing the potential of relief or gain. You are choosing to move forward, thus getting this guidebook, yet feelings of hopelessness still haunt you in covert (and sometimes overt) ways. You have received support from a therapist or you're considering doing so. You're still hoping to heal some aspects on your own terms and within your own*

No matter whether you're experiencing one or elements of all four scenarios, you whole-heartedly understand that you need a significant shift in your life. No exceptions. Your sense of thriving can no longer be in the form of you constantly "doing" only to be left feeling anxious, stressed and depleted. You now need to thrive in a way that gives you a sense of flow and authenticity. You are ready to be inspired, guided and reminded of your true worth which was given to you at birth without reservations. You have the key inside and this guidebook is here to teach you how to use it to unlock and find your voice in a new and innovative manner while considering your soul's purpose, strengths, barriers, challenges, thoughts, goals and much more.

PURPOSE OF THIS GUIDEBOOK SERIES

As someone who has suffered through each of these scenarios as well as being an educator and holistic health, wellness and THRIVE coach, I completely understand the need for guidance when change is required. For over a decade, I've been intentional with many aspects of my personal development due to experiencing a low-grade depression in my mid-30s. While I wasn't clinically depressed, I was at the lowest point of my adulthood thus far and needed a seismic shift to pivot me towards a new life experience. I chose to focus on my spiritual development, and my journey began in 2009. After feeling almost all elements of the aforementioned four scenarios, I realized I was experiencing rock bottom and I needed help. I was in therapy but it was only helping a part of my sense of self. I was coping, but not thriving. After years of therapy and still feeling stuck, I recognized that my soul wasn't being fed. In desperation, I asked God to lead me somewhere deeper, and the feelings I received in response to my request was that I needed to go away, retreat and learn something new about my soul. I completed an intense 4-day spiritual retreat and it was the beginning of my rebirth. I finally had a better sense of myself and could begin to thrive. However, that was just the first step in a life-long journey.

We must be willing to become life-long learners to promote continued growth and development. The intent of this guidebook is to create a safe space and process for you to do your own personal "retreat" by getting still, reflecting and discerning more about what is your actual voice versus the story and narrative that have resulted due to limited beliefs, fears and insecurities. Those are conditions, they are not your truth. Yet, they cause our beautifully inspired voices to be dampened, neglected and forgotten. This guidebook is formatted in a way to help you visit aspects of your life and not only determine how to thrive, but also how to nurture your constantly evolving self. If you are going to thrive, be inspired and live the life your soul came to live, you must take action in a supportive manner. Without proper support, any challenge has the potential to overwhelm your sensibilities. This guidebook is a tool to support you overcome those challenges.

HOW TO USE THE SEASON OF INTENTION GUIDEBOOK

While the guidebook series' purpose is to inspire you to thrive, it is organized in a manner that will continually prompt you to reflect on your unique qualities, contributions and abilities in order to establish a more meaningful life that is aligned with your personal needs. Before we delve into how to use the guidebook, it is important to establish a working definition of the word "thrive." According to Webster's dictionary, it means "prosper; flourish." This is a direct and simple definition that is suitable for how you should define "thrive" while using this guidebook. The opposite of the word thrive is decline, wither, fail or stagnate. If you are feeling any or all of these antonyms for thriving, you've landed in the right place. It is your time to shine! And, it's time for your soul and purpose to flourish.

The complete series of guidebooks is organized in a manner that provides you with "12 Principles to Thrive." These principles will allow you to create a blueprint for unlocking a part of yourself that needs nurturing in order for you to experience greater flow and motivation, which ultimately leads to you having a flourishing mindset. With this mindset, you will feel more empowered to take action with the intent of creating a lifestyle you desire.

Each individual guidebook allows you to explore your mindset, thoughts, habits and goals on a weekly basis. Every four weeks (approximately every month), you will explore one "principle to thrive". You will do daily activities that encourage you to rest, meditate, reflect on your strengths, identify your challenges, establish new behaviors, play and create a gratitude practice for your weekly dedication to self-growth. You simply follow the prompts each week and allow yourself to connect with what is being revealed.

This guidebook is titled "Season of Intention" and focuses on the following three principles:

- *Choose the life you want and live it!*

- *Give and receive love*

- *Establish safe spaces to be your whole self*

Each week, you will explore and rank a different affirmation related to the principle of the month. Counter to the traditional way of simply restating affirmations, you will have the opportunity to adjust and rewrite the affirmation so that it is more relevant to you and your level of personal growth and development. The guidebook provides prompts to assist as you rewrite each affirmation so that it is a realistic action which will help you thrive and develop.

What should you do when you are too busy or you simply don't have the energy to work on "self"? That is completely fine and is to be expected! My only request is that, at a minimum, you begin. You can always pick up where you left off when you're ready. It's important that you move through the guidebook with an abundant mindset. Often, the conditions that are placed upon us cause a scarcity mindset mainly because of the way we are taught to value aspects of life that have nothing to do with our personal truth. Given the state of the world and its often chaotic circumstances, you can feel removed from what you want due to simply "surviving" the challenges of life. We are not taught how to mend our wounds using small steps towards healing and building healthier lifestyle habits. Disease, illness and other stressors become the results of us being out of flow and lacking a sense of groundedness. In order to have greater emotional stability and peace of mind, it's imperative that you are intentional with your actions and that you create meaningful time to get still, reflect and receive what your intuition teaches you daily. You must listen to yourself to begin the process of personal growth. You must also trust what you hear, and only then you can truly take actions to in order to thrive according to your soul's purpose. Therefore, be patient and give yourself grace in the process of using each guidebook.

By now, you see that there are four different guidebooks according to the "season" you're currently in or wanting to embark on: Season of Intention, Season of Growth, Season of Reset, and Season of Rest. Irrespective of the season you have chosen, the guidebook is used in the same way; there are simply different thrive principles in each seasonal guidebook. If you decide to spend one month following the "Season of Growth" and then want to pivot to the "Season of Rest," feel free to do so. It is important that you utilize your power to choose and change your mind. Not getting fixed to one thing that begins to feel restrictive is a crucial aspect of thriving and will help you gain a sense of flow. You are beginning a journey of learning how to listen to and trust your intuition. Therefore, don't be surprised if you're compelled to switch to different seasons routinely.

In summary, *S.H.E. Guide to Thrive* is created to support you in becoming the best version of yourself. Be sure to take your time. The process of following the guidebooks will reveal both covert and overt changes. Some revelations and changes will be obvious while other aspects may not be revealed until much later. Simply know that by following the "12 Principles to Thrive" and engaging in the guidebook's introspective activities, you are strengthening a muscle that already exists. You're remembering YOU! Are you excited to begin? I am excited for you and am sending you abundant love and light. Enjoy the journey toward thriving!

As you begin the **First week** of reflection working towards this season of intention and transformation, the guiding principle is: *Choose the Life You Want & Live It.* For the next four weeks you will unpack and recreate personal affirmations that empower you within this principle.

Reflect, initiate, and thrive into your season of intention!

SUNDAY

MENTAL HEALTH CHECK IN

DATE

HOW ARE YOU FEELING TODAY?

HOW ARE YOU FEELING TODAY?

HOW CAN YOU IMPROVE YOUR MENTAL HEALTH

WHAT HAVE BEEN YOUR THREE DOMINANT EMOTIONS THIS WEEK?

▸

▸

▸

WHAT DO YOU FEEL GOOD ABOUT RIGHT NOW?

THINGS THAT TRIGGER NEGATIVE EMOTIONS

▸

▸

▸

▸

MY RANKING OF MY HEALTH THIS WEEK

☆☆☆☆☆

MONDAY

AFFIRMATION OF THE WEEK:
I create the life I desire.

ACTIVITY:

Rate on a scale from 0 to 5 how much you believe in or are currently doing this week's affirmation.

5 = ALWAYS	3 = SOMETIMES	1 = NOT REALLY
4 = MOST TIMES	2 = OCCASIONALLY	0 = NEVER

RATING: ___

REFLECTION ACTIVITY:

In order to make this week's affirmation more believable, relatable and one that will eventually allow you to thrive, you will be prompted to rewrite the affirmation by choosing one of the phrases below:

"I am working towards…"	"I am practicing…"
"I am determined to…"	"It is safe for me to…"

JOURNAL PROMPT:

Which phrase will you select from above to make this week's affirmation more believable and doable for you?

Rewrite your new affirmation, state it out loud and then reflect on why you selected your phrase.

REWRITTEN AFFIRMATION:

TUESDAY

What do you currently do that supports this week's affirmation (provide examples)?

REFLECT/JOURNAL:

WEDNESDAY

Which challenge prevents or hinders you from this week's affirmation (provide examples)?

REFLECT/JOURNAL:

THURSDAY

#THURSDAYTHRIVE OVERCOMING THE CHALLENGES & REMOVING THE BARRIERS

What support do you need & what actions will you take to better practice this week's affirmation?

REFLECT/JOURNAL:

FRIDAY

Choose a fun activity just for you.

BANK OF FUN ACTIVITIES:

Brain-dump through free writing

Declutter phone photos, vids

Unfollow people on social media

Do regular gratitude practice

Sit outside & do nothing

Schedule regular time off work (PTO)

Set a date for decluttering

Listen to a podcast

Use a meditation app

Journal

Go for a walk

Cook a new recipe

See a holistic practitioner, such as acupuncturist, naturopath, chiropractor

Take a cooking class

Drive on back roads

Go on a solo date

Enjoy a healthy snack in your favorite cafe

Sip on veggie/fruit water, such as lemon & cucumber, lime & berries

Work on a puzzle

Meditate/pray

Unsubscribe from unused email lists

Play loud music and dance to the rhythm without posting on social media

Declutter phone apps

Open window blinds daily even when its cloudy

Practice self-massage

Color/paint

Light a candle

Set a hot bath or shower date

Take deep breaths

Schedule and/or plan power naps

SATURDAY

FREE THOUGHT/DRAW, COMMENTS, GOALS, QUESTIONS, PLANS, etc.:

SUNDAY

MENTAL HEALTH CHECK IN

DATE

HOW ARE YOU FEELING TODAY?

HOW ARE YOU FEELING TODAY?

HOW CAN YOU IMPROVE YOUR MENTAL HEALTH

WHAT HAVE BEEN YOUR THREE DOMINANT EMOTIONS THIS WEEK?

▶

▶

▶

WHAT DO YOU FEEL GOOD ABOUT RIGHT NOW?

THINGS THAT TRIGGER NEGATIVE EMOTIONS

▶

▶

▶

▶

MY RANKING OF MY HEALTH THIS WEEK

☆ ☆ ☆ ☆ ☆

MONDAY

AFFIRMATION OF THE WEEK:
I choose me first.

ACTIVITY:

Rate on a scale from 0 to 5 how much you believe in or are currently doing this week's affirmation.

5 = ALWAYS   3 = SOMETIMES   1 = NOT REALLY
4 = MOST TIMES   2 = OCCASIONALLY   0 = NEVER

RATING: ___

REFLECTION ACTIVITY:

In order to make this week's affirmation more believable, relatable and one that will eventually allow you to thrive, you will be prompted to rewrite the affirmation by choosing one of the phrases below:

"I am working towards…"   "I am practicing…"
"I am determined to…"   "It is safe for me to…"

JOURNAL PROMPT:

Which phrase will you select from above to make this week's affirmation more believable and doable for you?

Rewrite your new affirmation, state it out loud and then reflect on why you selected your phrase.

REWRITTEN AFFIRMATION:

TUESDAY

What do you currently do that supports this week's affirmation (provide examples)?

REFLECT/JOURNAL:

WEDNESDAY

Which challenge prevents or hinders you from this week's affirmation (provide examples)?

REFLECT/JOURNAL:

THURSDAY

#THURSDAYTHRIVE OVERCOMING THE CHALLENGES & REMOVING THE BARRIERS

What support do you need & what actions will you take to better practice this week's affirmation?

REFLECT/JOURNAL:

FRIDAY

Choose a fun activity just for you.

BANK OF FUN ACTIVITIES:

Brain-dump through free writing

Declutter phone photos, vids

Unfollow people on social media

Do regular gratitude practice

Sit outside & do nothing

Schedule regular time off work (PTO)

Set a date for decluttering

Listen to a podcast

Use a meditation app

Journal

Go for a walk

Cook a new recipe

See a holistic practitioner, such as acupuncturist, naturopath, chiropractor

Take a cooking class

Drive on back roads

Go on a solo date

Enjoy a healthy snack in your favorite cafe

Sip on veggie/fruit water, such as lemon & cucumber, lime & berries

Work on a puzzle

Meditate/pray

Unsubscribe from unused email lists

Play loud music and dance to the rhythm without posting on social media

Declutter phone apps

Open window blinds daily even when its cloudy

Practice self-massage

Color/paint

Light a candle

Set a hot bath or shower date

Take deep breaths

Schedule and/or plan power naps

SATURDAY

GRATITUDE AND END OF WEEK

FREE THOUGHT/DRAW, COMMENTS, GOALS, QUESTIONS, PLANS, etc.:

SUNDAY

MENTAL HEALTH CHECK IN

DATE

HOW ARE YOU FEELING TODAY?

HOW ARE YOU FEELING TODAY?

HOW CAN YOU IMPROVE YOUR MENTAL HEALTH

WHAT HAVE BEEN YOUR THREE DOMINANT EMOTIONS THIS WEEK?

▸

▸

▸

WHAT DO YOU FEEL GOOD ABOUT RIGHT NOW?

THINGS THAT TRIGGER NEGATIVE EMOTIONS

▸

▸

▸

▸

MY RANKING OF MY HEALTH THIS WEEK

MONDAY

AFFIRMATION OF THE WEEK:
I make my life abundant.

ACTIVITY:

Rate on a scale from 0 to 5 how much you believe in or are currently doing this week's affirmation.

5 = ALWAYS	3 = SOMETIMES	1 = NOT REALLY
4 = MOST TIMES	2 = OCCASIONALLY	0 = NEVER

RATING: ___

REFLECTION ACTIVITY:

In order to make this week's affirmation more believable, relatable and one that will eventually allow you to thrive, you will be prompted to rewrite the affirmation by choosing one of the phrases below:

"I am working towards…"   "I am practicing…"
"I am determined to…"   "It is safe for me to…"

JOURNAL PROMPT:

Which phrase will you select from above to make this week's affirmation more believable and doable for you?

Rewrite your new affirmation, state it out loud and then reflect on why you selected your phrase.

REWRITTEN AFFIRMATION:

TUESDAY

What do you currently do that supports this week's affirmation (provide examples)?

REFLECT/JOURNAL:

WEDNESDAY

Which challenge prevents or hinders you from this week's affirmation (provide examples)?

REFLECT/JOURNAL:

THURSDAY

What support do you need & what actions will you take to better practice this week's affirmation?

REFLECT/JOURNAL:

FRIDAY

Choose a fun activity just for you.

BANK OF FUN ACTIVITIES:

Brain-dump through free writing

Declutter phone photos, vids

Unfollow people on social media

Do regular gratitude practice

Sit outside & do nothing

Schedule regular time off work (PTO)

Set a date for decluttering

Listen to a podcast

Use a meditation app

Journal

Go for a walk

Cook a new recipe

See a holistic practitioner, such as acupuncturist, naturopath, chiropractor

Take a cooking class

Drive on back roads

Go on a solo date

Enjoy a healthy snack in your favorite cafe

Sip on veggie/fruit water, such as lemon & cucumber, lime & berries

Work on a puzzle

Meditate/pray

Unsubscribe from unused email lists

Play loud music and dance to the rhythm without posting on social media

Declutter phone apps

Open window blinds daily even when its cloudy

Practice self-massage

Color/paint

Light a candle

Set a hot bath or shower date

Take deep breaths

Schedule and/or plan power naps

SATURDAY

FREE THOUGHT/DRAW, COMMENTS, GOALS, QUESTIONS, PLANS, etc.:

SUNDAY

MENTAL HEALTH CHECK IN

DATE

HOW ARE YOU FEELING TODAY?

HOW ARE YOU FEELING TODAY?

HOW CAN YOU IMPROVE YOUR MENTAL HEALTH

WHAT HAVE BEEN YOUR THREE DOMINANT EMOTIONS THIS WEEK?

▸

▸

▸

WHAT DO YOU FEEL GOOD ABOUT RIGHT NOW?

THINGS THAT TRIGGER NEGATIVE EMOTIONS

▸

▸

▸

▸

MY RANKING OF MY HEALTH THIS WEEK

☆ ☆ ☆ ☆ ☆

MONDAY

AFFIRMATION OF THE WEEK:
I release what does not serve my life in a positive manner.

ACTIVITY:

Rate on a scale from 0 to 5 how much you believe in or are currently doing this week's affirmation.

5 = ALWAYS   3 = SOMETIMES   1 = NOT REALLY
4 = MOST TIMES   2 = OCCASIONALLY   0 = NEVER

RATING: ___

REFLECTION ACTIVITY:

In order to make this week's affirmation more believable, relatable and one that will eventually allow you to thrive, you will be prompted to rewrite the affirmation by choosing one of the phrases below:

"I am working towards…"   "I am practicing…"
"I am determined to…"   "It is safe for me to…"

JOURNAL PROMPT:

Which phrase will you select from above to make this week's affirmation more believable and doable for you?

Rewrite your new affirmation, state it out loud and then reflect on why you selected your phrase.

REWRITTEN AFFIRMATION:

TUESDAY

What do you currently do that supports this week's affirmation (provide examples)?

REFLECT/JOURNAL:

WEDNESDAY

Which challenge prevents or hinders you from this week's affirmation (provide examples)?

REFLECT/JOURNAL:

THURSDAY

What support do you need & what actions will you take to better practice this week's affirmation?

REFLECT/JOURNAL:

FRIDAY

CELEBRATE YOU!

Choose a fun activity just for you.

BANK OF FUN ACTIVITIES:

Brain-dump through free writing

Declutter phone photos, vids

Unfollow people on social media

Do regular gratitude practice

Sit outside & do nothing

Schedule regular time off work (PTO)

Set a date for decluttering

Listen to a podcast

Use a meditation app

Journal

Go for a walk

Cook a new recipe

See a holistic practitioner, such as acupuncturist, naturopath, chiropractor

Take a cooking class

Drive on back roads

Go on a solo date

Enjoy a healthy snack in your favorite cafe

Sip on veggie/fruit water, such as lemon & cucumber, lime & berries

Work on a puzzle

Meditate/pray

Unsubscribe from unused email lists

Play loud music and dance to the rhythm without posting on social media

Declutter phone apps

Open window blinds daily even when its cloudy

Practice self-massage

Color/paint

Light a candle

Set a hot bath or shower date

Take deep breaths

Schedule and/or plan power naps

SATURDAY

FREE THOUGHT/DRAW, COMMENTS, GOALS, QUESTIONS, PLANS, etc.:

As you begin the **Fifth week** of reflection working towards this season of intention and transformation, the next guiding principle is *Give & Receive Love.* For the next four weeks you will unpack and recreate personal affirmations that empower you within this principle.

Reflect, initiate, and thrive into your season of intention!

SUNDAY

MENTAL HEALTH CHECK IN

DATE

HOW ARE YOU FEELING TODAY?

HOW ARE YOU FEELING TODAY?

HOW CAN YOU IMPROVE YOUR MENTAL HEALTH

WHAT HAVE BEEN YOUR THREE DOMINANT EMOTIONS THIS WEEK?

▶

▶

▶

WHAT DO YOU FEEL GOOD ABOUT RIGHT NOW?

THINGS THAT TRIGGER NEGATIVE EMOTIONS

▶

▶

▶

▶

MY RANKING OF MY HEALTH THIS WEEK

☆ ☆ ☆ ☆ ☆

MONDAY

AFFIRMATION OF THE WEEK:

I give compassion to myself as I do unto others.

ACTIVITY:

Rate on a scale from 0 to 5 how much you believe in or are currently doing this week's affirmation.

5 = ALWAYS	3 = SOMETIMES	1 = NOT REALLY
4 = MOST TIMES	2 = OCCASIONALLY	0 = NEVER

RATING: ___

REFLECTION ACTIVITY:

In order to make this week's affirmation more believable, relatable and one that will eventually allow you to thrive, you will be prompted to rewrite the affirmation by choosing one of the phrases below:

"I am working towards…"   "I am practicing…"
"I am determined to…"   "It is safe for me to…"

JOURNAL PROMPT:

Which phrase will you select from above to make this week's affirmation more believable and doable for you?

Rewrite your new affirmation, state it out loud and then reflect on why you selected your phrase.

REWRITTEN AFFIRMATION:

TUESDAY

What do you currently do that supports this week's affirmation (provide examples)?

REFLECT/JOURNAL:

WEDNESDAY

PERSONAL INQUIRY

Which challenge prevents or hinders you from this week's affirmation (provide examples)?

REFLECT/JOURNAL:

THURSDAY

What support do you need & what actions will you take to better practice this week's affirmation?

REFLECT/JOURNAL:

FRIDAY

Choose a fun activity just for you.

BANK OF FUN ACTIVITIES:

Brain-dump through free writing

Declutter phone photos, vids

Unfollow people on social media

Do regular gratitude practice

Sit outside & do nothing

Schedule regular time off work (PTO)

Set a date for decluttering

Listen to a podcast

Use a meditation app

Journal

Go for a walk

Cook a new recipe

See a holistic practitioner, such as acupuncturist, naturopath, chiropractor

Take a cooking class

Drive on back roads

Go on a solo date

Enjoy a healthy snack in your favorite cafe

Sip on veggie/fruit water, such as lemon & cucumber, lime & berries

Work on a puzzle

Meditate/pray

Unsubscribe from unused email lists

Play loud music and dance to the rhythm without posting on social media

Declutter phone apps

Open window blinds daily even when its cloudy

Practice self-massage

Color/paint

Light a candle

Set a hot bath or shower date

Take deep breaths

Schedule and/or plan power naps

SATURDAY

FREE THOUGHT/DRAW, COMMENTS, GOALS, QUESTIONS, PLANS, etc.:

SUNDAY

MENTAL HEALTH CHECK IN

DATE
____

HOW ARE YOU FEELING TODAY?

HOW ARE YOU FEELING TODAY?

HOW CAN YOU IMPROVE YOUR MENTAL HEALTH

WHAT HAVE BEEN YOUR THREE DOMINANT EMOTIONS THIS WEEK?

▸ _______________________

▸ _______________________

▸ _______________________

WHAT DO YOU FEEL GOOD ABOUT RIGHT NOW?

THINGS THAT TRIGGER NEGATIVE EMOTIONS

▸ _______________________

▸ _______________________

▸ _______________________

▸ _______________________

MY RANKING OF MY HEALTH THIS WEEK

☆ ☆ ☆ ☆ ☆

MONDAY

AFFIRMATION OF THE WEEK:
*I receive compassion wholeheartedly
when others give it to me.*

ACTIVITY:

Rate on a scale from 0 to 5 how much you believe in or are currently doing this week's affirmation.

5 = ALWAYS   3 = SOMETIMES   1 = NOT REALLY
4 = MOST TIMES   2 = OCCASIONALLY   0 = NEVER

RATING: ___

REFLECTION ACTIVITY:

In order to make this week's affirmation more believable, relatable and one that will eventually allow you to thrive, you will be prompted to rewrite the affirmation by choosing one of the phrases below:

"I am working towards…"   "I am practicing…"
"I am determined to…"   "It is safe for me to…"

JOURNAL PROMPT:

Which phrase will you select from above to make this week's affirmation more believable and doable for you?

Rewrite your new affirmation, state it out loud and then reflect on why you selected your phrase.

REWRITTEN AFFIRMATION:

TUESDAY

What do you currently do that supports this week's affirmation (provide examples)?

REFLECT/JOURNAL:

WEDNESDAY

Which challenge prevents or hinders you from this week's affirmation (provide examples)?

REFLECT/JOURNAL:

THURSDAY

What support do you need & what actions will you take to better practice this week's affirmation?

REFLECT/JOURNAL:

FRIDAY

Choose a fun activity just for you.

BANK OF FUN ACTIVITIES:

Brain-dump through free writing

Declutter phone photos, vids

Unfollow people on social media

Do regular gratitude practice

Sit outside & do nothing

Schedule regular time off work (PTO)

Set a date for decluttering

Listen to a podcast

Use a meditation app

Journal

Go for a walk

Cook a new recipe

See a holistic practitioner, such as acupuncturist, naturopath, chiropractor

Take a cooking class

Drive on back roads

Go on a solo date

Enjoy a healthy snack in your favorite cafe

Sip on veggie/fruit water, such as lemon & cucumber, lime & berries

Work on a puzzle

Meditate/pray

Unsubscribe from unused email lists

Play loud music and dance to the rhythm without posting on social media

Declutter phone apps

Open window blinds daily even when its cloudy

Practice self-massage

Color/paint

Light a candle

Set a hot bath or shower date

Take deep breaths

Schedule and/or plan power naps

SATURDAY

FREE THOUGHT/DRAW, COMMENTS, GOALS, QUESTIONS, PLANS, etc.:

SUNDAY

MENTAL HEALTH CHECK IN

DATE

HOW ARE YOU FEELING TODAY?

HOW ARE YOU FEELING TODAY?

HOW CAN YOU IMPROVE YOUR MENTAL HEALTH

WHAT HAVE BEEN YOUR THREE DOMINANT EMOTIONS THIS WEEK?

▸

▸

▸

WHAT DO YOU FEEL GOOD ABOUT RIGHT NOW?

THINGS THAT TRIGGER NEGATIVE EMOTIONS

▸

▸

▸

▸

MY RANKING OF MY HEALTH THIS WEEK

☆ ☆ ☆ ☆ ☆

MONDAY

AFFIRMATION OF THE WEEK:
I am worthy of the love I desire.

ACTIVITY:

Rate on a scale from 0 to 5 how much you believe in or are currently doing this week's affirmation.

5 = ALWAYS	3 = SOMETIMES	1 = NOT REALLY
4 = MOST TIMES	2 = OCCASIONALLY	0 = NEVER

RATING: ___

REFLECTION ACTIVITY:

In order to make this week's affirmation more believable, relatable and one that will eventually allow you to thrive, you will be prompted to rewrite the affirmation by choosing one of the phrases below:

"I am working towards…"   "I am practicing…"
"I am determined to…"   "It is safe for me to…"

JOURNAL PROMPT:

Which phrase will you select from above to make this week's affirmation more believable and doable for you?

Rewrite your new affirmation, state it out loud and then reflect on why you selected your phrase.

REWRITTEN AFFIRMATION:

TUESDAY

What do you currently do that supports this week's affirmation (provide examples)?

REFLECT/JOURNAL:

WEDNESDAY

Which challenge prevents or hinders you from this week's affirmation (provide examples)?

REFLECT/JOURNAL:

THURSDAY

What support do you need & what actions will you take to better practice this week's affirmation?

REFLECT/JOURNAL:

FRIDAY

Choose a fun activity just for you.

BANK OF FUN ACTIVITIES:

Brain-dump through free writing

Declutter phone photos, vids

Unfollow people on social media

Do regular gratitude practice

Sit outside & do nothing

Schedule regular time off work (PTO)

Set a date for decluttering

Listen to a podcast

Use a meditation app

Journal

Go for a walk

Cook a new recipe

See a holistic practitioner, such as acupuncturist, naturopath, chiropractor

Take a cooking class

Drive on back roads

Go on a solo date

Enjoy a healthy snack in your favorite cafe

Sip on veggie/fruit water, such as lemon & cucumber, lime & berries

Work on a puzzle

Meditate/pray

Unsubscribe from unused email lists

Play loud music and dance to the rhythm without posting on social media

Declutter phone apps

Open window blinds daily even when its cloudy

Practice self-massage

Color/paint

Light a candle

Set a hot bath or shower date

Take deep breaths

Schedule and/or plan power naps

SATURDAY

FREE THOUGHT/DRAW, COMMENTS, GOALS, QUESTIONS, PLANS, etc.:

SUNDAY

MENTAL HEALTH CHECK IN

DATE

____

HOW ARE YOU FEELING TODAY?

HOW ARE YOU FEELING TODAY?

HOW CAN YOU IMPROVE YOUR MENTAL HEALTH

WHAT HAVE BEEN YOUR THREE DOMINANT EMOTIONS THIS WEEK?

▸ ___________________________

▸ ___________________________

▸ ___________________________

WHAT DO YOU FEEL GOOD ABOUT RIGHT NOW?

THINGS THAT TRIGGER NEGATIVE EMOTIONS

▸ ___________________________

▸ ___________________________

▸ ___________________________

▸ ___________________________

MY RANKING OF MY HEALTH THIS WEEK

☆ ☆ ☆ ☆ ☆

MONDAY

AFFIRMATION - STATE, RATE & REFLECT

AFFIRMATION OF THE WEEK:

I receive loving acts of kindness from others.

ACTIVITY:

Rate on a scale from 0 to 5 how much you believe in or are currently doing this week's affirmation.

5 = ALWAYS   3 = SOMETIMES   1 = NOT REALLY
4 = MOST TIMES   2 = OCCASIONALLY   0 = NEVER

RATING: ___

REFLECTION ACTIVITY:

In order to make this week's affirmation more believable, relatable and one that will eventually allow you to thrive, you will be prompted to rewrite the affirmation by choosing one of the phrases below:

"I am working towards…"   "I am practicing…"
"I am determined to…"   "It is safe for me to…"

JOURNAL PROMPT:

Which phrase will you select from above to make this week's affirmation more believable and doable for you?

Rewrite your new affirmation, state it out loud and then reflect on why you selected your phrase.

REWRITTEN AFFIRMATION:

TUESDAY

PERSONAL INQUIRY

What do you currently do that supports this week's affirmation (provide examples)?

REFLECT/JOURNAL:

WEDNESDAY

Which challenge prevents or hinders you from this week's affirmation (provide examples)?

REFLECT/JOURNAL:

THURSDAY

What support do you need & what actions will you take to better practice this week's affirmation?

REFLECT/JOURNAL:

FRIDAY

Choose a fun activity just for you.

BANK OF FUN ACTIVITIES:

Brain-dump through free writing

Declutter phone photos, vids

Unfollow people on social media

Do regular gratitude practice

Sit outside & do nothing

Schedule regular time off work (PTO)

Set a date for decluttering

Listen to a podcast

Use a meditation app

Journal

Go for a walk

Cook a new recipe

See a holistic practitioner, such as acupuncturist, naturopath, chiropractor

Take a cooking class

Drive on back roads

Go on a solo date

Enjoy a healthy snack in your favorite cafe

Sip on veggie/fruit water, such as lemon & cucumber, lime & berries

Work on a puzzle

Meditate/pray

Unsubscribe from unused email lists

Play loud music and dance to the rhythm without posting on social media

Declutter phone apps

Open window blinds daily even when its cloudy

Practice self-massage

Color/paint

Light a candle

Set a hot bath or shower date

Take deep breaths

Schedule and/or plan power naps

SATURDAY

FREE THOUGHT/DRAW, COMMENTS, GOALS, QUESTIONS, PLANS, etc.:

As you begin the **Ninth week** of reflection working towards this season of intention and transformation, the next guiding principle is *Establish Safe Spaces to be Your Whole Self.* For the next four weeks you will unpack and recreate personal affirmations that empower you within this principle.

Reflect, initiate, and thrive into your season of intention!

SUNDAY

MENTAL HEALTH CHECK IN

DATE

HOW ARE YOU FEELING TODAY?

HOW ARE YOU FEELING TODAY?

HOW CAN YOU IMPROVE YOUR MENTAL HEALTH

WHAT HAVE BEEN YOUR THREE DOMINANT EMOTIONS THIS WEEK?

▶

▶

▶

WHAT DO YOU FEEL GOOD ABOUT RIGHT NOW?

THINGS THAT TRIGGER NEGATIVE EMOTIONS

▶

▶

▶

▶

MY RANKING OF MY HEALTH THIS WEEK

☆ ☆ ☆ ☆ ☆

MONDAY

AFFIRMATION OF THE WEEK:
I make my home a sanctuary that reflects my whole self.

ACTIVITY:

Rate on a scale from 0 to 5 how much you believe in or are currently doing this week's affirmation.

5 = ALWAYS	3 = SOMETIMES	1 = NOT REALLY
4 = MOST TIMES	2 = OCCASIONALLY	0 = NEVER

RATING: ___

REFLECTION ACTIVITY:

In order to make this week's affirmation more believable, relatable and one that will eventually allow you to thrive, you will be prompted to rewrite the affirmation by choosing one of the phrases below:

"I am working towards…"   "I am practicing…"
"I am determined to…"   "It is safe for me to…"

JOURNAL PROMPT:

Which phrase will you select from above to make this week's affirmation more believable and doable for you?

Rewrite your new affirmation, state it out loud and then reflect on why you selected your phrase.

REWRITTEN AFFIRMATION:

TUESDAY

What do you currently do that supports this week's affirmation (provide examples)?

REFLECT/JOURNAL:

WEDNESDAY

Which challenge prevents or hinders you from this week's affirmation (provide examples)?

REFLECT/JOURNAL:

THURSDAY

What support do you need & what actions will you take to better practice this week's affirmation?

REFLECT/JOURNAL:

FRIDAY

Choose a fun activity just for you.

BANK OF FUN ACTIVITIES:

Brain-dump through free writing

Declutter phone photos, vids

Unfollow people on social media

Do regular gratitude practice

Sit outside & do nothing

Schedule regular time off work (PTO)

Set a date for decluttering

Listen to a podcast

Use a meditation app

Journal

Go for a walk

Cook a new recipe

See a holistic practitioner, such as acupuncturist, naturopath, chiropractor

Take a cooking class

Drive on back roads

Go on a solo date

Enjoy a healthy snack in your favorite cafe

Sip on veggie/fruit water, such as lemon & cucumber, lime & berries

Work on a puzzle

Meditate/pray

Unsubscribe from unused email lists

Play loud music and dance to the rhythm without posting on social media

Declutter phone apps

Open window blinds daily even when its cloudy

Practice self-massage

Color/paint

Light a candle

Set a hot bath or shower date

Take deep breaths

Schedule and/or plan power naps

SATURDAY

FREE THOUGHT/DRAW, COMMENTS, GOALS, QUESTIONS, PLANS, etc.:

SUNDAY

MENTAL HEALTH CHECK IN

DATE

HOW ARE YOU FEELING TODAY?

HOW ARE YOU FEELING TODAY?

HOW CAN YOU IMPROVE YOUR MENTAL HEALTH

WHAT HAVE BEEN YOUR THREE DOMINANT EMOTIONS THIS WEEK?

▸

▸

▸

WHAT DO YOU FEEL GOOD ABOUT RIGHT NOW?

THINGS THAT TRIGGER NEGATIVE EMOTIONS

▸

▸

▸

▸

MY RANKING OF MY HEALTH THIS WEEK

☆ ☆ ☆ ☆ ☆

MONDAY

AFFIRMATION OF THE WEEK:
I understand my whole self, and my values and beliefs.

ACTIVITY:

Rate on a scale from 0 to 5 how much you believe in or are currently doing this week's affirmation.

5 = ALWAYS	3 = SOMETIMES	1 = NOT REALLY
4 = MOST TIMES	2 = OCCASIONALLY	0 = NEVER

RATING: ___

REFLECTION ACTIVITY:

In order to make this week's affirmation more believable, relatable and one that will eventually allow you to thrive, you will be prompted to rewrite the affirmation by choosing one of the phrases below:

"I am working towards…"   "I am practicing…"
"I am determined to…"   "It is safe for me to…"

JOURNAL PROMPT:

Which phrase will you select from above to make this week's affirmation more believable and doable for you?

Rewrite your new affirmation, state it out loud and then reflect on why you selected your phrase.

REWRITTEN AFFIRMATION:

TUESDAY

What do you currently do that supports this week's affirmation (provide examples)?

REFLECT/JOURNAL:

WEDNESDAY

Which challenge prevents or hinders you from this week's affirmation (provide examples)?

REFLECT/JOURNAL:

THURSDAY

What support do you need & what actions will you take to better practice this week's affirmation?

REFLECT/JOURNAL:

FRIDAY

Choose a fun activity just for you.

BANK OF FUN ACTIVITIES:

Brain-dump through free writing

Declutter phone photos, vids

Unfollow people on social media

Do regular gratitude practice

Sit outside & do nothing

Schedule regular time off work (PTO)

Set a date for decluttering

Listen to a podcast

Use a meditation app

Journal

Go for a walk

Cook a new recipe

See a holistic practitioner, such as acupuncturist, naturopath, chiropractor

Take a cooking class

Drive on back roads

Go on a solo date

Enjoy a healthy snack in your favorite cafe

Sip on veggie/fruit water, such as lemon & cucumber, lime & berries

Work on a puzzle

Meditate/pray

Unsubscribe from unused email lists

Play loud music and dance to the rhythm without posting on social media

Declutter phone apps

Open window blinds daily even when its cloudy

Practice self-massage

Color/paint

Light a candle

Set a hot bath or shower date

Take deep breaths

Schedule and/or plan power naps

SATURDAY

FREE THOUGHT/DRAW, COMMENTS, GOALS, QUESTIONS, PLANS, etc.:

SUNDAY

MENTAL HEALTH CHECK IN

DATE

HOW ARE YOU FEELING TODAY?

HOW ARE YOU FEELING TODAY?

HOW CAN YOU IMPROVE YOUR MENTAL HEALTH

WHAT HAVE BEEN YOUR THREE DOMINANT EMOTIONS THIS WEEK?

-
-
-

WHAT DO YOU FEEL GOOD ABOUT RIGHT NOW?

THINGS THAT TRIGGER NEGATIVE EMOTIONS

-
-
-
-

MY RANKING OF MY HEALTH THIS WEEK

☆☆☆☆☆

MONDAY

AFFIRMATION OF THE WEEK:
I make my relationships safe so that I can feel whole within them.

ACTIVITY:

Rate on a scale from 0 to 5 how much you believe in or are currently doing this week's affirmation.

5 = ALWAYS   3 = SOMETIMES   1 = NOT REALLY
4 = MOST TIMES   2 = OCCASIONALLY   0 = NEVER

RATING: ___

REFLECTION ACTIVITY:

In order to make this week's affirmation more believable, relatable and one that will eventually allow you to thrive, you will be prompted to rewrite the affirmation by choosing one of the phrases below:

"I am working towards…"   "I am practicing…"
"I am determined to…"   "It is safe for me to…"

JOURNAL PROMPT:

Which phrase will you select from above to make this week's affirmation more believable and doable for you?

Rewrite your new affirmation, state it out loud and then reflect on why you selected your phrase.

REWRITTEN AFFIRMATION:

TUESDAY

What do you currently do that supports this week's affirmation (provide examples)?

REFLECT/JOURNAL:

WEDNESDAY

"Which challenge prevents or hinders you from this week's affirmation (provide examples)?"

REFLECT/JOURNAL:

THURSDAY

What support do you need & what actions will you take to better practice this week's affirmation?

REFLECT/JOURNAL:

FRIDAY

Choose a fun activity just for you.

BANK OF FUN ACTIVITIES:

Brain-dump through free writing

Declutter phone photos, vids

Unfollow people on social media

Do regular gratitude practice

Sit outside & do nothing

Schedule regular time off work (PTO)

Set a date for decluttering

Listen to a podcast

Use a meditation app

Journal

Go for a walk

Cook a new recipe

See a holistic practitioner, such as acupuncturist, naturopath, chiropractor

Take a cooking class

Drive on back roads

Go on a solo date

Enjoy a healthy snack in your favorite cafe

Sip on veggie/fruit water, such as lemon & cucumber, lime & berries

Work on a puzzle

Meditate/pray

Unsubscribe from unused email lists

Play loud music and dance to the rhythm without posting on social media

Declutter phone apps

Open window blinds daily even when its cloudy

Practice self-massage

Color/paint

Light a candle

Set a hot bath or shower date

Take deep breaths

Schedule and/or plan power naps

SATURDAY

FREE THOUGHT/DRAW, COMMENTS, GOALS, QUESTIONS, PLANS, etc.:

SUNDAY

MENTAL HEALTH CHECK IN

DATE

HOW ARE YOU FEELING TODAY?

HOW ARE YOU FEELING TODAY?

HOW CAN YOU IMPROVE YOUR MENTAL HEALTH

WHAT HAVE BEEN YOUR THREE DOMINANT EMOTIONS THIS WEEK?

▶

▶

▶

WHAT DO YOU FEEL GOOD ABOUT RIGHT NOW?

THINGS THAT TRIGGER NEGATIVE EMOTIONS

▶

▶

▶

▶

MY RANKING OF MY HEALTH THIS WEEK

☆ ☆ ☆ ☆ ☆

MONDAY

AFFIRMATION OF THE WEEK:
I can trust myself.

ACTIVITY:

Rate on a scale from 0 to 5 how much you believe in or are currently doing this week's affirmation.

5 = ALWAYS   3 = SOMETIMES   1 = NOT REALLY
4 = MOST TIMES   2 = OCCASIONALLY   0 = NEVER

RATING: ___

REFLECTION ACTIVITY:

In order to make this week's affirmation more believable, relatable and one that will eventually allow you to thrive, you will be prompted to rewrite the affirmation by choosing one of the phrases below:

"I am working towards..."   "I am practicing..."
"I am determined to..."   "It is safe for me to..."

JOURNAL PROMPT:

Which phrase will you select from above to make this week's affirmation more believable and doable for you?

Rewrite your new affirmation, state it out loud and then reflect on why you selected your phrase.

REWRITTEN AFFIRMATION:

TUESDAY

What do you currently do that supports this week's affirmation (provide examples)?

REFLECT/JOURNAL:

WEDNESDAY

Which challenge prevents or hinders you from this week's affirmation (provide examples)?

REFLECT/JOURNAL:

THURSDAY

#THURSDAYTHRIVE OVERCOMING THE CHALLENGES & REMOVING THE BARRIERS

What support do you need & what actions will you take to better practice this week's affirmation?

REFLECT/JOURNAL:

FRIDAY

Choose a fun activity just for you.

BANK OF FUN ACTIVITIES:

Brain-dump through free writing

Declutter phone photos, vids

Unfollow people on social media

Do regular gratitude practice

Sit outside & do nothing

Schedule regular time off work (PTO)

Set a date for decluttering

Listen to a podcast

Use a meditation app

Journal

Go for a walk

Cook a new recipe

See a holistic practitioner, such as acupuncturist, naturopath, chiropractor

Take a cooking class

Drive on back roads

Go on a solo date

Enjoy a healthy snack in your favorite cafe

Sip on veggie/fruit water, such as lemon & cucumber, lime & berries

Work on a puzzle

Meditate/pray

Unsubscribe from unused email lists

Play loud music and dance to the rhythm without posting on social media

Declutter phone apps

Open window blinds daily even when its cloudy

Practice self-massage

Color/paint

Light a candle

Set a hot bath or shower date

Take deep breaths

Schedule and/or plan power naps

SATURDAY

FREE THOUGHT/DRAW, COMMENTS, GOALS, QUESTIONS, PLANS, etc.:

KENYA MCGUIRE JOHNSON

Kenya McGuire Johnson, PT, MA, CHC is the Owner & Founder of Finding Your Voice Health & Wellness. As an artist, creative entrepreneur, astrology self-care coach and certified holistic wellness coach, she wears many hats, yet her overall purpose is within the healing arts.

As a coach and former practicing physical therapist, she provides strategies that help diverse women thrive and create a transformative mindset while manifesting a meaningful lifestyle. A graduate of Howard University, Kenya is also on faculty and Director of Student Development & Diversity, Equity & Inclusion programming in the College of Health Sciences at Rush University in Chicago, IL.

When she is not counseling or coaching, she is producing and hosting the podcast Finding Your Voice After 40 as well as overseeing KenyaMJ Music Productions, LLC which includes her healing arts' services and retreats.

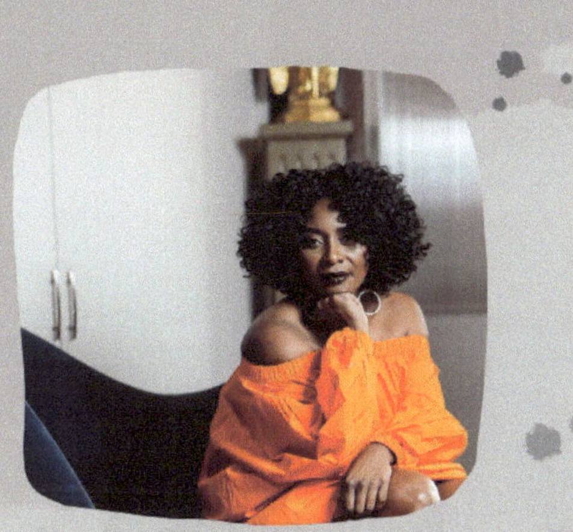